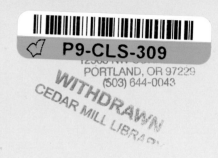

To Justin —B.H.

The illustrations in this book were done in pen and ink, watercolor, and digital media.

The text type was set in Agenda and Felt-Tip Woman.
The display type was hand-lettered by David Clark.

Library of Congress Cataloging-in-Publication Data
Heos, Bridget, author.
Just like us!, ants / by Bridget Heos.
pages cm
Summary: "Just Like Us! Ants gives young readers an up-close and personal look at how ants
do things that are remarkably similar to the way humans do." — Provided by publisher.
Audience: Ages 4–8.
Audience: K to grade 3.
Includes bibliographical references.
ISBN 978-0-544-57043-6
1. Ants—Juvenile literature. 2. Ants—Behavior—Juvenile literature. I. Title. II. Title: Ants.
QL568.F7H46 2016
595.79'6—dc23
2015018892

Manufactured in Malaysia
TWP 10 9 8 7 6 5 4 3 2 1
4500660119

Lexile Level	Guided Reading	Fountas & Pinnell	Interest Level
840	R	P	Grades K–2

JUST LIKE US! ANTS

by **Bridget Heos**

illustrated by **David Clark**

HOUGHTON MIFFLIN HARCOURT

Boston   New York

DID YOU KNOW that ants have been farming for longer than humans? And that in addition to raising crops, they herd (and milk) animals? Ants also build roads, sew, and construct rafts to survive floods. In these and other ways, ants are just like us. Read on to learn more about these fantastic, or rather ANT-astic, insects.

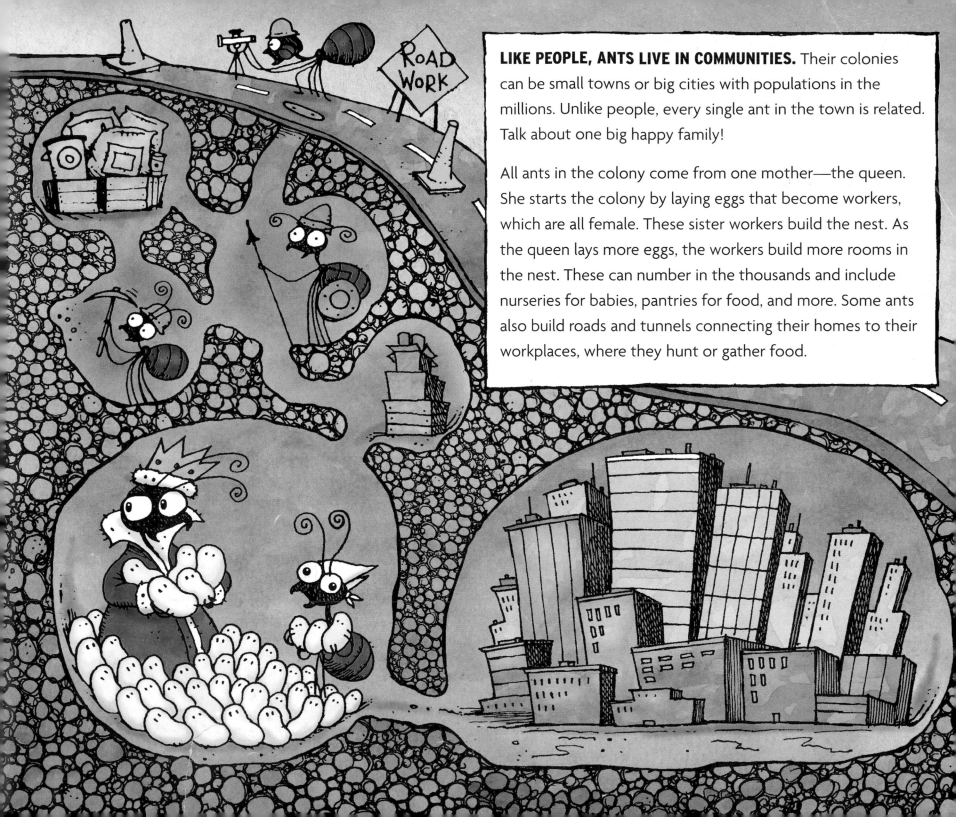

LIKE PEOPLE, ANTS LIVE IN COMMUNITIES. Their colonies can be small towns or big cities with populations in the millions. Unlike people, every single ant in the town is related. Talk about one big happy family!

All ants in the colony come from one mother—the queen. She starts the colony by laying eggs that become workers, which are all female. These sister workers build the nest. As the queen lays more eggs, the workers build more rooms in the nest. These can number in the thousands and include nurseries for babies, pantries for food, and more. Some ants also build roads and tunnels connecting their homes to their workplaces, where they hunt or gather food.

BUG EAT BUG JOB

LIKE PEOPLE, ANTS WORK HARD AT THEIR JOBS. Some ants keep their job their whole lives. However, in many species, ants change jobs as they get older.

Young adult **harvester ants** work safely inside the nest. They may be garbage workers, carrying seed husks to the nearby dump. Or they may join the construction crew, fixing collapsed walls and adding on new rooms. As they get older, they get promoted to collecting seeds outside the nest, where there is always the threat of other insects attacking. It's a dangerous job. But an ant's got to eat!

GOOD BABY~~SITTERS~~ CRITTERS

AN ANT'S FIRST JOB is often to babysit her little sisters (which are tiny, ricelike worms called larvae). Babysitter ants feed the babies by chewing up food and spitting it into their mouths. They give the babies baths by licking them with sticky saliva. And they protect them by carrying them deeper into the nest when danger strikes.

Queen's Feast The same babysitter ants that feed the larvae also feed the queen, who is too busy laying eggs to do anything else. They spit the food into her mouth, too. For ants, it's a meal fit for a queen! Or should we say *spit* for a queen?

Ewwww

I Vant to Suck Your Bug Juice While some ants feed their babies, other ants feed **on** them! **Dracula ants** bite their larvae and drink their blood. The larvae somehow survive this, but it's still not very nice. Less painful but no less weird, **Leptanilla** larvae have a spigot that adult ants drink from like a straw.

SOME ANT BABIES HELP OUT TOO—with dinner! **Bigheaded ants** catch fruit flies. But since the fruit flies won't fit through the ants' tiny digestive tracts, the ants give them to their larvae. The babies drool on the flies, turning them into mush (or protein shakes), which the grownups can then digest. The babies slurp the shakes too, but only after the grownups have dined. Age before larvae!

ANT FARM

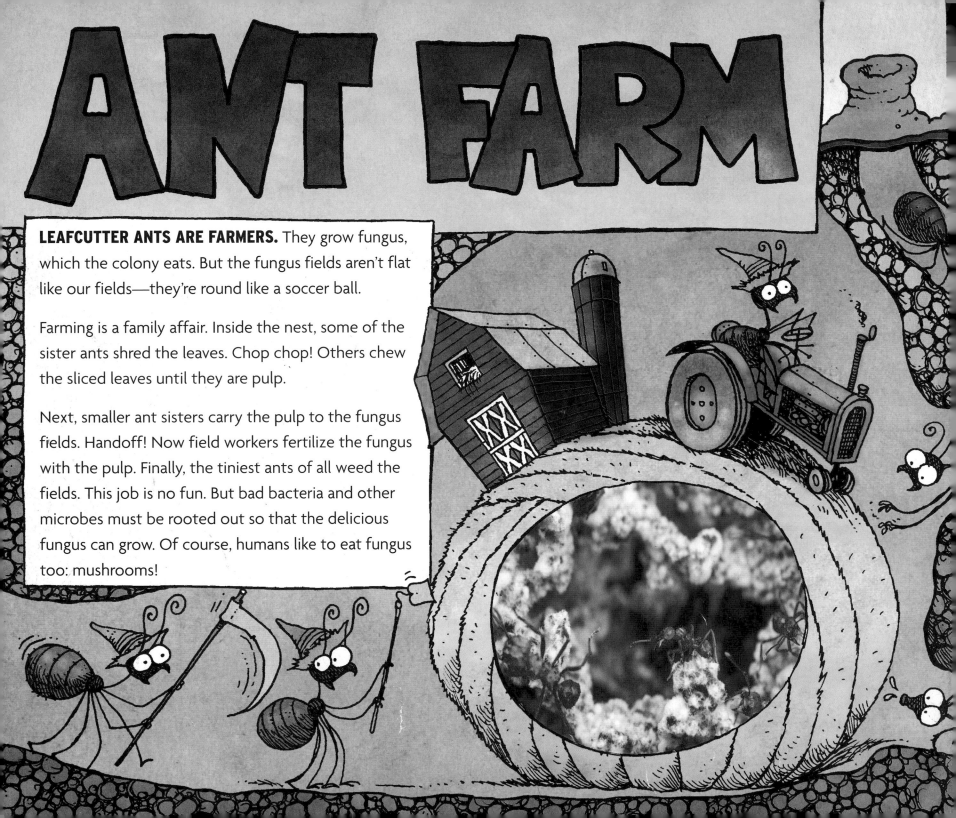

LEAFCUTTER ANTS ARE FARMERS. They grow fungus, which the colony eats. But the fungus fields aren't flat like our fields—they're round like a soccer ball.

Farming is a family affair. Inside the nest, some of the sister ants shred the leaves. Chop chop! Others chew the sliced leaves until they are pulp.

Next, smaller ant sisters carry the pulp to the fungus fields. Handoff! Now field workers fertilize the fungus with the pulp. Finally, the tiniest ants of all weed the fields. This job is no fun. But bad bacteria and other microbes must be rooted out so that the delicious fungus can grow. Of course, humans like to eat fungus too: mushrooms!

IT'S A DIRTY JOB, BUT SOMEBUGGY'S GOT TO DO IT

AFTER THE FIELDS ARE WEEDED, a new group of ants carries the weeds to the dump. These ants are like hazmat workers because some of the weeds are deadly—or *haz*ardous *mat*erials. Unfortunately, there are no hazmat suits to protect the ants. Worse, once they've started working, the other ants won't let the hazmat team near the fungus fields, to avoid contamination. So the selfless workers must eat what they find in the trash. It's a tragic fate.

WEAVER ANTS ARE DAIRY FARMERS. Only instead of cattle, they raise tiny insects called mealy bugs. The mealy bugs are corralled in pens made of leaves. When the mealy bugs have sucked all the sap from the leaves in one pen, the ants herd the little insects to a new pen. Similar to farmers milking cows, weaver ants "milk" mealy bugs. The ants rub the bugs' bellies, and the mealy bugs poop out a honeylike substance called manna. The ants feed it to their baby sisters. As with dairy cows, milking does not hurt the mealy bugs. But the baby ants love it! "Thanks for the mealy bug poop, kind sisters!"

DON'T LOSE YOUR HEAD IN TRAFFIC!

JUST LIKE PEOPLE, ants must deal with traffic on their way to work. A leafcutter's job is to collect leaves to fertilize their crops. With strong, sharp jaws called mandibles, they slice off sections of leaves and carry them back to the nest. Each piece is three times the ant's weight. The ants *could* carry even more, but wider loads would cause traffic jams. And if traffic slowed too much, the ants would be in danger. Flies often loom overhead. If they manage to land on a leaf and lay an egg in the ant's mouth, the maggot will hatch and eat the ant's brain, causing its head to fall off. This brings a whole new meaning to rush hour!

NO WIDE LOADS

POP!

DANG!...

KEEP UP SPEED

Living Fly Swatters Leafcutter ants take an extra precaution to avoid losing their heads in traffic jams. They have tiny ants ride along on the leaves they carry. These little ants swat away the flies. It pays to have friends in high places!

KILL the BEAST!

DURING THE LAST ICE AGE, humans hunted in packs to bring down mammoths. Ants bring down animals even larger, proportionally. **Azteca andreae ants** can kill an insect 13,350 times their size. That would be like human hunters killing a two-million-pound land animal, or a beast the size of twenty brachiosauruses, with their bare hands.

The hunting grounds of *Azteca andreae* ants are leaves. While some of the ants hold the giant insect still, the others make the kill. It's difficult to capture such a giant beast without falling off the leaf. The ants use Velcro-like hooks on their feet so that they don't lose their footing.

SEW HOMEY

WEAVER ANTS SEW LEAVES together with thread. But instead of making clothing, they sew their homes! First, the ants pull two leaves together. They hold on to one another at the waist and form a chain that spans the leaves. One by one, the ants hop off the ant chain, shortening the distance between the two leaves. When the leaves nearly touch, an ant holds a larva. The ant zigzags back and forth between the leaves. Sticky silk comes out of the baby's mouth. Now the leaves are sewn together. The sewn leaves become a leaf house that protects the ants from rain. The forest canopy is filled with leaf homes, at the middle of which are the precious queen and her babies.

Nice Threads! Having silk squeezed out of it doesn't hurt the larva. It will later spin a cocoon with the same silk. Inside, the larva metamorphoses (transforms) into an adult ant.

Ants Sweet Ants: There's no need for army ants to sew their own homes. Their nests are made of the ants themselves. They are called bivonacs. The queen and her larvae are tucked safely in the center of the million living ants that make up the bivonac.

BRIDGE CLUB

AN ANT CAN FALL FROM ANY HEIGHT and not get hurt. But climbing back up the tree is a long and treacherous journey. That's why to get to a neighboring tree, weaver ants build bridges. The bridges are made of the ants themselves. Ants in opposite trees form chains by holding one another at the waist. The ants at the tips of the two chains reach for each other, linking the bridge.

ALL IN THE SAME BOAT

PEOPLE HAVE BUILT RAFTS for thousands of years. But ants have built rafts for *millions* of years. What material do they use? Themselves! During a flood, fire ants grab one another's legs with their claws or jaws. Air bubbles trapped between their bodies allow them all to float on the water as a group.

Ant rafts more closely resemble the rubber rafts of today than the log rafts of old. The weave of their bodies acts like waterproof fabric. If you were to press down on the center of an ant raft, it would bounce right back up.

THIS MEANS WAR!

ANTS CONSTANTLY WAGE WAR on neighboring colonies. For instance, **fire ants** know that where there is a **woodland ant** nest, there is food. And so they plan their attack. First, the fire ants send out a scout to find the woodland ant nest. The scout rubs her belly along the trail on her way back home. This lays down scents called pheromones, which ants use to communicate. In this case, the pheromones lead the scout's nest-mates to the battlefield and tell them to attack.

On the battlefield, woodland soldiers use their mandibles like swords against the enemy. But the fire ants outnumber the woodland ants a hundredfold, and soon close in on their nest. As a last-ditch effort, the woodland soldiers form a line at their nest's entrance and fight to the death. This buys their sisters time to escape. But the battle is lost. The victorious fire ants steal food from the woodland ant nest, then flee. When the woodland ants return home, they must gather all new food and raise new larvae to become brave soldiers.

Smell You Later! Inside the nest, the other woodland ants sound the alarm about the attack by rubbing their tummies on the ground. This pheromone says, "Run! Save the babies! Save yourselves!" The queen and workers, carrying the larvae, flee.

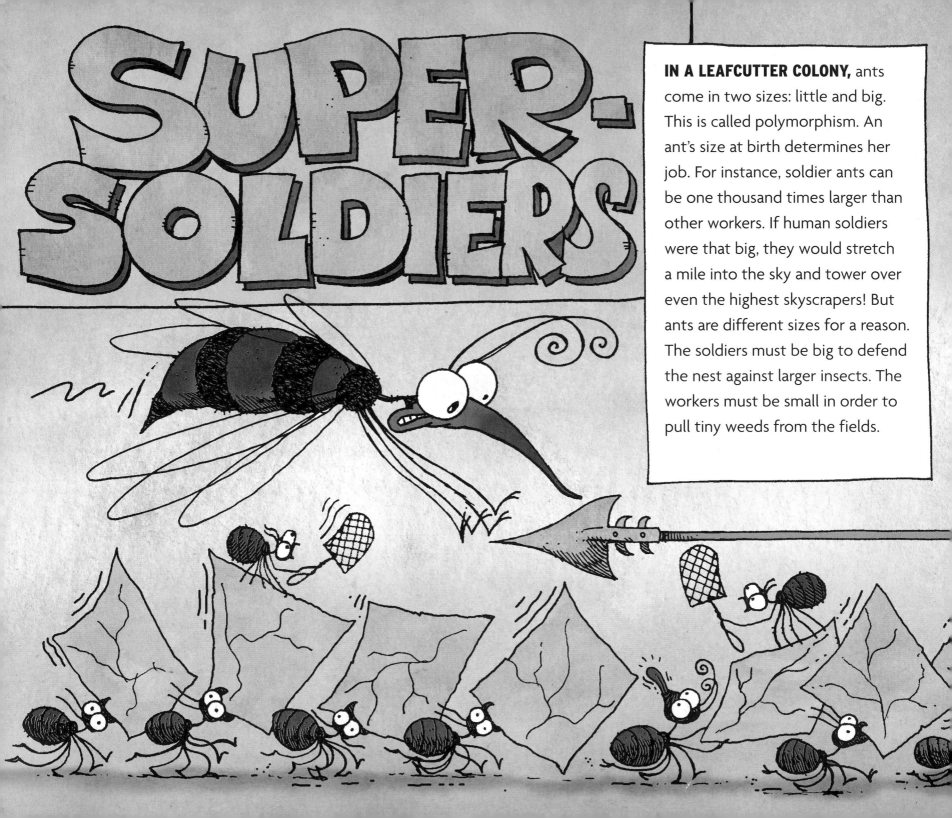

SUPER-SOLDIERS

IN A LEAFCUTTER COLONY, ants come in two sizes: little and big. This is called polymorphism. An ant's size at birth determines her job. For instance, soldier ants can be one thousand times larger than other workers. If human soldiers were that big, they would stretch a mile into the sky and tower over even the highest skyscrapers! But ants are different sizes for a reason. The soldiers must be big to defend the nest against larger insects. The workers must be small in order to pull tiny weeds from the fields.

INDIVIDUAL ANTS PERISH EVERY DAY—whether from war, drought, flooding, or even a fateful footstep. Yet the ant family lives on.

For a short time each year, a small number of larvae metamorphose into males and queens. These winged ants mate. The males die soon after. But just as people sometimes leave their hometowns, the queens fly off to new places. There they found new colonies.

They lay eggs, which hatch into larvae. The queen cares for the first group of larvae herself. When the babies become adults, they take over the babysitting duties. Meanwhile, the queen has more and more babies, who all grow up to be hard workers. They build the city, protect their fellow ants, and gather food to share. And the circle of life continues for the ants, who are just like us.

...and So do ANTS

SAY WHAT?

bacteria single-celled organisms, some of which can cause diseases in ants.

bivouacs ant nests made of the ants themselves.

brachiosaurus a large herbivorous dinosaur.

cocoon a silk casing spun by some insect larvae, inside which they transform into adult insects.

colony a community of ants that share a queen and live and work together to find food and protect themselves.

fungus an organism that reproduces by use of spores, and feeds on leaves and other organic matter. It is neither a plant nor an animal, but is more closely related to animals.

hazmat short for *hazardous material,* or waste that can cause disease or injury.

larvae baby ants, which look like wriggly grains of rice.

maggot a baby fly.

mammoths hairy elephants that lived during the ice age and are now extinct.

mandibles an ant's sharp jaws, used as tools for slicing food and weapons for fighting.

manna a honeylike substance excreted by mealy bugs.

metamorphose to transform from a wormlike baby insect into an adult.

microbes organisms that can only be seen under a microscope.

nest the structure in which ants live. It can be made of many different materials, including leaves, the dirt underground, and even the ants themselves.

pheromones a scent excreted by ants to communicate with other ants.

polymorphism a noticeable difference in size among specific groups of animals from the same species.

queen the mother of all ants in a colony.

sap the liquid that circulates throughout plants.

workers all female ants other than the queen. They perform all of the work in the colony.

BIBLIOGRAPHY

Choi, Charles. "Ants Use Velcro Claws to Ambush Heavy Prey." *Live Science*, June 30, 2010.
   (www.livescience.com/6653-ants-velcro-claws-ambush-heavy-prey.html)

"Fire Ants Surf Floods on Rafts of Their Own Bodies." *AAAS Science*, April 25, 2011.
   (news.sciencemag.org/2011/04/fire-ants-surf-floods-rafts-their-own-bodies)

Gordon, Deborah. *Ants at Work*. New York: Simon and Schuster, 1999.

Hölldobler, Bert, and Edward O. Wilson. *Journey to the Ants*. Cambridge: Harvard University Press, 1994.

Hoyt, Erich. *The Earth Dwellers*. New York: Simon and Schuster, 1996.

Mlot, Nathan. "A Fire Ant Ball Is Pushed Under Water 2." April 20, 2010.
   (www.youtube.com/watch?v=Oujgzk8sHWk)

Moffett, Mark. *Adventures Among Ants*. Berkeley: University of California Press, 2010.

Texas Parks and Wildlife. "Nature's Bath Time."
   (www.tpwd.state.tx.us/publications/nonpwdpubs/young_naturalist/animals/natures_bath_time)

BRIDGET HEOS is the author of more than sixty nonfiction titles for kids and teens, including *Shell, Beak, Tusk; Stronger Than Steel; It's Getting Hot in Here; I Fly;* and *What to Expect When You're Expecting Larvae.* She's also the author of the picture books *Mustache Baby,* and *Mustache Baby Meets His Match.* Bridget lives in Kansas City with her husband and four children, and you can learn more about her and her books at authorbridgetheos.com.

DAVID CLARK has illustrated numerous picture books including *Pirate Bob, Fractions in Disguise,* and *The Mine-o-Saur.* He also co-created—and illustrates—the nationally syndicated comic strip Barney & Clyde. David lives in Virginia with his family, and you can learn more about his books and his comics at sites.google.com/site/davidclark1988.

Photo Credits: Alex Wild, pages 4, 6, 9–10, 13, 14, 16, 18, 20–22, 25, 28